THE ABSENCE OF YOU

ANNIE SOPHIE LE

Copyright © 2021 by Annie Sophie Le

All rights reserved.

No part of this book may be reproduced in any form or by any electronic or mechanical means, including information storage and retrieval systems, without written permission from the author, except for the use of brief quotations in a book review.

ISBN: 978-1-7775696-0-0

CONTENTS

Raincloud Umbrella	1
Sunny Side Up	2
The Weight of Depression	3
You Are Not Here	5
Pillow Thoughts I	7
Skipping Days	8
Absent	10
Casualties	11
Are We Contagious?	14
Magic Trick	15
Troubled	17
Tiny Burdens	18
Hollowed	20
Stuck	21
The Cave	22
Lonely Hearts	23
Lost at Sea	24
Missing	25
Sleeping with the Fishes	27
Aloneness	28
War	29
Missing Poster	32
There	33
Isolation Tank	34
Haunting You	36
The Sharpness of Nostalgia	38
Tomb	40
Taking Up Space	42
Diplomacy of Broken Hearts	43
Greasy Hair and Dirty Pyjamas	45
Ocean of Salt	47
The Insomniacs Club	48
Destroy Yourself	49

The Dichotomy of Being Here and Being Gone	50
Shrine	51
One Day at a Time	52
Faithful Disconsolation	53
Alone	54
Doubtful	55
Youngblood	56
Pillow Thoughts II	57
Depression	58
Winter	59
Lost in Healing	60
Claustrophobic Love	61
Equation	63
Here is the Catch-22	64
Monstrous	65
Dreaming Away	66
Rose-Tinted Glasses	67
Even Together, We're Far Apart	68
Friends Turned Strangers	69
Glassine Words	71
The Grace in Being Sad	72
Cadmean Victory	74
Unwell	75
Sleeping Away	76
The Mourning	77
Blue	78
Impostor	79
Pink Elephant	80
Teeth	81
Starstruck	83
Hope for the Hopeless	84
You Are Not Weak for Needing Help	86
The Finery of Hope	87
Coming Alive	88
Corporeal	90
Reprieve	91
Acknowledgments	93

THE ABSENCE OF YOU

RAINCLOUD UMBRELLA

Maybe you're just having a bad day, they say,
but you can tell the difference
between a drizzle and a hurricane.

SUNNY SIDE UP

You tell them you're fine,
everything is turning up sunny,

repeat it over and over,
hoping the words will stick
to your skin and bloom into truths.

You tell yourself you're okay,
finally on the mend,

repeat it over and over,
hoping there'll come a day
when you finally believe it.

THE WEIGHT OF DEPRESSION

I.
Your friends stop coming around, a burden and a relief.
You wish they would keep trying to reach you,
climb the glass tower you built to rescue you,
but you want them to let you sleep, leave you to the dragon.
When you are together, you wonder,
Am I here or am I invisible?
 Do I exist or am I an imaginary friend?

II.
When you speak, you weave words together,
hoping your friends will understand
this new strange language.
The distance grows between your smiles,
and you both ignore the elephantine silences
that fill the space between your words.
When you together, you aren't really there,
you fade in and out and wonder,
When will they leave me?
When can I leave myself?

III.
Your friends stop coming around, grow tired
of your depression.
You understand their silence
and make love to your loneliness.
How could they ever like you
when you don't even like yourself?
You've taken their laughter and smiles from them,
sucking their bones dry,
until they too become lifeless and colourless
just like you.

YOU ARE NOT HERE

They see your smile
but not the sadness it is built upon.
They hear your words that you are fine,
but not the truth that hides
in the spaces between the words.

You are falling apart, imploding inwards,
a cataclysmic display
of hurricane madness and waterfall tears.

To hold yourself together, you wrap yourself in twigs,
hoping you can make it through another day
with this makeshift skin.

Even now,
you are fighting this war against yourself,
knowing there will be a day
when your feet will falter and the madness
will come calling you home,

and it is like this,
you are tumbling back down.

You are not yourself,
you are not here.

PILLOW THOUGHTS I

Are you tired

or are you sad?

SKIPPING DAYS

How could they ever understand
the weight of melancholy
tugging at your limbs,
anchored to your ankles,
pulling you down
into an ocean of shame,
of tear-stained pillows,
and fingernails bitten and chewed
in a fit of anxiety?

You dream of getting up
and blooming like wildflowers,
but instead, lose yourself
to the barren winter of your sadness.

The world forgets about you,
the depressed, the ill, the hopeless.
You are faceless in a sea of nobodies,
reduced to a disorder
you must recite to doctors and specialists
even before your name,
institutionalized and disregarded,
no humanity, no dignity.

Only when someone cracks and disappears
does the world speak hollow words,
telling you to simply reach out for help.
If only it were that simple.
If only the invisible were made visible.

ABSENT

The silences carry
the absence of you.
Your smiles carry
the absence of light.

CASUALTIES

We lose so much of ourselves to the darkness in our minds, to our sadness, to our illness, and when we finally shake off the fog, we are left to look around at the barrenness of our lives, what remains after being ravaged. It is a war we fight, year after year, for so long. We don't remember how it feels to like ourselves, to know ourselves, to be anything but ill.

We are veterans of warring minds and troubled hearts. We want peace, but even we don't know what that means. We look around after the bombs have stopped tumbling from the skies, a lull in the chaos, and take inventory of what remains. We have gained knowledge and wisdom, born from pain, but we have lost so much. Too much. We have lost those who can't weather our storms; we lose others to the time and the distance we place between them and us. Missed chances and lost opportunities, choking on all of the things we could have done, all the people we could have loved, but instead, we suffocated in the cocoons of illness. So we grieve; what else can we do but grieve? Should we rage against the illness, throw our hands in the air at the unfairness of it all?

. . .

Some may never understand but those of us who are old and weathered, veterans of emotional hurricanes and tsunamis, understand. We know there are some that are the lucky ones, and we, we are the unlucky. Lucky ones, living scenes plucked from movies that tell tales of love and laughter, pages ripped from books that whisper of adventures had and lives fulfilled. We are Sleeping Beauties, sleeping when others dance, losing ourselves where others are found, stumbling when others run, beautiful in our brokenness.

We look around and realize we have learned so much but at what cost? The cost of our lives and our hearts? We can never have nostalgia for the best years of our lives. We have spent years being wrapped in our illnesses, years hiding under the covers, years starving ourselves for perfection we will never reach, years cutting ourselves to pieces, years in comas, years lost to trying times.

Our realities stopped because of our illnesses, but the world didn't. Others moved on and replaced us from their lives. Some have castles and some have sailboats, taking them far away from here. But what do we have? Scarred hearts and dashed hopes.

The world is spinning all around us, people rushing by, a blurred bokeh of colours. Voices chatter in languages of life and happiness, in languages we only dream of one day knowing, but we are lost in translation. We are standing in quicksand while others buzz and flicker around us, busily running from dream to smile and back again.

. . .

We mourn for all we lost, for all we never had. We mourn for ourselves and hope, hope one day we will know ourselves, intimately and wholly, just as we know every line and edge of our sadness.

ARE WE CONTAGIOUS?

Why is it so easy
for passersby
to move around you
when you are stumbling
with outstretched arms
for someone to reach out
and steady you?

MAGIC TRICK

Are you uncomfortable around people,
or are you afraid of what they'll see
when they look at you?
Unable to meet the gazes of the faces you talk to,

you've forgotten how to speak,
only remembering the language of the broken.
You've forgotten how to live, other than just getting by.
Every syllable and sound, every movement and glance,
uncomfortable and unnerving.

You are an alien—
in your own skin, in your surroundings.
You aren't present, not here, not anymore,
you've spent too long in your coma of loneliness,
in the cocoon of your illness.

You don't see a problem with hiding away.
You've found your sanctuary
and you're never really alone,
not with your melancholy to keep you company.

But you've made a pillow fort in a cage,

covered the bars with blankets, until you've forgotten,
this is your prison.
Now, even when you leave the cage

and step into the scurrying crowds,
you are frozen while they move around you,
stuck on pause while they are on fast forward.

When you meet with friends, they can't reach you.
You are beside them, but you aren't really there.
Your friends feel like strangers now.
Even you
are a stranger to yourself,

and when words flow from their mouths,
you fade from the conversation,
wondering if you're fading right before their eyes.
Will they see your magic trick
of vanishing into the air?

TROUBLED

our hearts are homeless

TINY BURDENS

They think you can heal
and move on from your mental illness,
that it's behind you and in the past,
the struggle is over, and you'll never fall ill again.
It's this pressure they place on your shoulders,
a blanket smothering you, a burden so heavy
you wonder if your knees will crack,
a failed Atlas.

You aren't depressed today?
They assume your depression, a dragon,
has been slain forever.
You hurt yourself before?
They think you've moved on, lessons learned,
and will never fall into the darkness again.
It's these lies they tell themselves,
strings they tie around your limbs,
parading you around, a prized fish
they'll gut and hang above their mantlepiece.

Then you find yourself lost in the fog again,
relapse biting at your heels. These are our lives
for the ill, the survivors, the healed.

The darkness is inevitable, lurking around us,
waiting, always waiting,
and when you struggle, you keep it to yourself,
not wanting to disappoint those
who pressure you with their tiny burdens.

If only they knew,
this exhaustive battling in your head,
inescapable thoughts you can never outrun.
It's like this,
the pressure under your skin
builds and builds,
and it's like this,
you find yourself wondering,
can you be strong to face another day?

HOLLOWED

Who are you
without
the madness
and
the melancholy?

STUCK

It is here,
in the moments
between careful words
and searching gazes
where you struggle to hide
a watery nose and leaking eyes,
shifting
shifting
shifting
unsure if you were
always this way
or if your sadness
turned you into this.

THE CAVE

There are days when you think
you are getting better,
only to slip and fall.

There are days when you think
you are getting worse,
only to feel the lightness of the sun.

Does this wariness scare you
into using it as an excuse
to never change and grow?
Or are you fragile and about to break
at the slightest of words?

This unknowing—
their caution, your isolation,
becomes too much.

And just when you thought
you had grappled your way
out of the cave,
you realize all you did was descend
further into the darkness.

LONELY HEARTS

I.
    We are hollow, we are full,
    under the pressure we put on ourselves
    to be perfect, to be enough, to be someone else.

II.
    We are hollow, we are full,
    abandoned hearts and reaching fingers,
    always wanting but too scared to hold on.

III.
    We are hollow, we are full,
    when will we be enough for ourselves,
    when will our lonely hearts and diseased hopes
    turn hopeful and loving?

LOST AT SEA

The lost,
the broken,
the damaged
will understand how it feels

to be here but not be here,
to be a ghost and an echo
while your body remains
and your mind floats away.

To feel invisible,
despite being surrounded by others,
and feel a growing distance

between them and you,
between life and you,
and knowing
no one can reach you.

You're sailing away
right before their eyes.

MISSING

You are frustrated
in your struggle to feel, to relate to others.
You aren't present, you aren't here,
and even when you are, your eyes
can't hold their gazes, too worried
they'll see the truth.

Don't know if you're alive.
Don't know who you are.
Don't know where you are.
Don't know don't know don't know.

You can't rustle up enthusiasm, though you try,
your voice monotone and monochromatic,
matching the grey you feel, the grey you see.
You try to keep the conversation alive,
but you forget how, your words tumbling
to the floor, crashing at your feet,
as the silence pushes you away from them.

You hate this,
hate unknowing, hate how you aren't here,
hate how you feel like a forgery of a person, a con man,

despite your best attempts at being yourself,
whoever the hell you are.
You mimic their movements, you repeat their words,
just so they don't see your plastic skin,
a faceless mannequin.

It is painful to be alone
when you are with the ones you love,
and it's like this,
you start to resent them, begin to hate them
for reminding you of what you've lost
and can never get back.
You start to resent yourself, begin to hate yourself
for feeling like this, ashamed of what you've become.

You're stuck in this rut, just stuck,
unable to speak because they don't speak
the same language, and you know they'll leave,
grow tired of translating.
But still, you try and try and try,
chatting but not looking in their eyes,
lost in your thoughts,

and suddenly,
you don't feel anything for them
besides the numbness that swallowed you whole,
a whale swallowing the sea.
How do you forgive yourself for losing them
like you lost yourself?

SLEEPING WITH THE FISHES

They mean well—
oh, how they mean well,
but good intentions
are cinderblock shoes.

ALONENESS

You feel so alone sometimes,
wondering if they miss you
when even your shadow has left.

You sit on your bed of madness,
chewing loneliness in the silence,
and the silence speaks to you,
telling you tales of your childhood,
before the madness descended,
the times when you were happy and alive.

And when your madness finds you,
cowering under your bed,
you hug it to your heart
and just like this,
you aren't alone anymore.

WAR

I.
You are lost in translation, mid-conversation,
stuck acting out a scene, doing your part,
until you can flee and get away
from them
from this
from here.
This is what depression is, this is what illness is,
whatever your diagnosis, even if you don't have one,
whatever the colour of your un-wellness is.
This is what it feels like
to be lost in your own body,
missing from your own life.

II.
Even when you wake, you aren't really awake.
You've lost, a casualty in this war against yourself,
and you mourn those who
couldn't deal
didn't reach for you
didn't understand
grew tired of you always being sick

left before you could wake.
It never feels quite the same as it once did,
before the bombs dropped from the sky,
before the tornado came, eating all in its path.

III.
The friends you had before the war
are no longer friends, they are strangers now.
It's hard to be with them, harder to relate and feel
as you once did.
There are a few who remain, but even they
are scarred from the war.
Then there are the friends you made
during the gunfire and after the fog cleared.
They are closer to you, saw you covered
in blood and mud, stuck and caged,
a prisoner of war.

IV.
So you let go, let go of the ones before,
let go of the nostalgia that tries to pull you back,
and when you reach out,
you feel like an impostor in your own skin.
You don't belong back there,
not with the people before the war.
But you hold on—or at least try to,
to your comrades and fellow veterans of the warring.
It is easier to be with them, the silence comfortable.
You are at ease with each other,
shell-shocked but alive.

V.
Words flow now,
hands reach out and grasp desperately.
You both share the same language

of the damaged and the endured,
the brave and the survived.
At least here,
you belong.

MISSING POSTER

You've disappeared
from your own life,
and you wonder,
do you even exist?

THERE

You write a makeshift list
on a scrap of wrinkled yellowing paper,
scribble a catalogue of all of the medications
you take daily, wondering how much longer
this will go on, this ritual of trying to get better,
to fix the chemical imbalance in your brain.
And when you visit your doctor, handing over
the list of synthetic chemicals that
keep you upright,
you lose yourself in the monotone words
of *How are you doing?* and *I'm fine*,
bitterly aware that you have been reduced
to a medical interaction,
not human, not alive,
just there.

ISOLATION TANK

It is a dinner party
with bubbling laughter and pounding music
but you are surrounded
by missing ears and muted mouths.
When arms are open wide,
even well-meaning words hurt.

You walk around in circles,
sizing up your opponent.
You don't want to fight but you do,
sparring back and forth,
hurricane words from lashing tongues.
Your intent isn't to maim
or cut their limbs from their bodies.
You simply want to emphasize your heart
stitched to your chest,
but even your best attempts at connecting
disembowel them.

It is confinement, this isolation around you,
a sweater too small you squeeze into,
leaving you with sweating limbs,
twisted in limbo.

Even innocent words hurt
sympathetic reaching hands.

The ones outside the wildness
will cut their fingers and toes
to try and fit on your bed of madness,
wanting to understand, but they can't,
not when they don't speak the same language
or share the same madness.

Only the disordered and the lost
will share the same bed,
exchanging crooked smiles and morbid jokes,
carrying a red mark slashed
across their chests for all to see,
speaking the same language
of twisted fingers in trying times.

You will find space to flourish
in the sameness of being unwell,
and here,
there is freedom.

HAUNTING YOU

They don't know what it's like
to have a diagnosis, or to search for one,
blind to the ghost floating behind you.
And when they speak, their consoling words
deflect on your armour of neurosis.

When you tell them they don't understand
this haunting of you,
they take offence, carrying hurt in their arms,
a weight too heavy to sustain.

And you are burdened
with your ghost following you around,
speaking in tongues that worry and scare.

All you want is someone to hear
and understand you, to be known,
your ghost acknowledged.
So you surround yourself
with the broken and the mended,

and you will be seen—

not just in pieces and fragments,
but entirely and completely.

THE SHARPNESS OF NOSTALGIA

Remember when our childhoods
were hand-me-downs and scabbed knees?
There wasn't a tree we wouldn't climb,
our pockets weighted with rocks and hand-picked flowers,
our appetites endless, fingers sticky with sweets.

Remember when we felt too much and sang too loud,
on the verge of tears or laughter,
either happy or heartsick, wanting or gloomy,
flying high or tumbling down, but never walking,
our momentum always forward?

Remember when our beds were never made,
our hair tangled and wild,
fingernails dirty from mud-pies?
We would build sandcastles in the playground,
surrounded by moats so wide
no one could touch us.

Remember when we were so tiny, and yet,
our fingers skimmed the clouds? If we reached a little more,
we could have caught them in our hands,
our dreams bigger than our little bodies.

We were unstoppable, always believing we could,
the possibilities endless. Even the monsters under our beds
were afraid of us.

Remember when hope came easy and believing was simple,
dreams painless, brave hearts young and carefree?
We shrugged away our fears and leapt without looking,
promises made between best friends, sealed with twisted little
fingers.
We would never be defeated, or lose our dreams to the world,
when we used to like ourselves and who we wanted to be.

Remember when we used to feel alive?

TOMB

When they leave, you tell yourself you don't care,
firmly and with conviction,
but you know your conviction is a shallow river,
never quite touching, never quite reaching
the dark place inside
where you bury your little secrets
under layers of guilt and shame.
You don't care, not one bit, not at all,
but it's too late. You've made a career
as a mathematician and archeologist.

You've measured the details, the quantity of misplaced tears
and mapped the days when being invisible
was the only thing that kept you upright,
tracing and excavating where you began
and your sadness ended.
Hours spent sitting on your bed, in the company of silence,
in the white noise of an unwatched television,
you followed the red string connecting you to them,
finding only the frayed edge, the ending.

You deciphered the text messages, calculated the words
that came quickly and faded to nothing,

you could have written books
tracing the lineage of your love,
the way it blossomed from two nobodies,
into a magnificent secret culture
only the two of you shared.

You tell yourself you don't miss them, you don't care,
it's a lie you tell yourself, over and over,
hoping the words will stick to your tongue,
become your truth.
There was a time when the two of you
were inseparable, lips touching, hands grasping,
sinking into each other until your skins melded together.
When you were with them,
they could have studied your bones
and seen how deeply embedded the two of you were.

Not anymore.
Now, if they ripped you open to study your guts,
all they would find is a hollowed-out hole,
emptied out, no vibrancy of life,
and absent of you.

TAKING UP SPACE

In television shows and in movies,
mental illness is romantic and beautiful,
reduced to stereotypes,
a manic pixie girl, a cute depressed boy.

But when you take up space,
you and your illness,
you become an attraction,
ugly and disgusting.

You no longer have your dignity,
being sensationalized and demonized,
nothing more than a totem
for them to carry in their pockets,
showing you off as their prized possession.

If only they would see you as a person,
acknowledge your humanity,
and you would tell them,
this is what mental illness looks like.

DIPLOMACY OF BROKEN HEARTS

You are sitting across from each other, staring,
trying to decipher each other's faces,
the table between you becoming a canyon,
the distance growing and growing.

You are ambassadors from different lands,
one at war and one in bloom,
speaking different languages,
the getting-by and the thriving.

There was a time, before the volcano erupted,
when you were close, when love came easily,
a field of flowering hearts and blooming smiles.

But after the ash of depression settles, there is distance,
withering the hearts and freezing the smiles,
until they are the sun, and you are the moon,
lightness and darkness,
the presence of them, the absence of you.

You want mutual destruction, taking them
down with you, so petty and frustrated,
but they move on, letting go,

and you are stuck, holding on.

Instead,
you settle on diplomacy,
cutting your losses and retreating,
deciding to release them
and bury your dead.

GREASY HAIR AND DIRTY PYJAMAS

Grief isn't a pretty little thing.
It isn't tidy, it won't fit into a box with a shiny red bow,
it's a rabid three-headed dog that turns on itself,
seeping from your marrow, burning through your veins,
waiting, lurking in your peripherals, always out of sight,
biding its time for the moment when you think
you can survive this.
Then it flitters back, grinning its toothless smile,
slipping back inside you.
Your lungs burn, the air too weighted,
heavy with all of your what-ifs and should-haves.

The walls become your lover. They keep you company
when no one else will,
bearing witness to your tears, never turning away
from your stained pyjamas and matted hair.
Just be, they whisper, even when you don't want to go on.
When your heart is splitting apart and you shatter
into fireworks of tears,
you go on, moving forward, when all you want is to go back.
Despite yourself, you go on, you breathe,
betraying yourself by enduring, by surviving.

There are pieces of you, lost and missing, limbs you can't regrow,
but layer by layer, you rebuild yourself.

They say grief will get easier in time, so you wait
and wait and wait
but it doesn't get easier, the easy days are gone.
You're not okay, not now, not anymore,
but still, you wait.

You survived the loss, the ashes slipping
through your fingertips,
dancing in the wind and leaving you behind.
It's a study in pain, to face the quietness of the night
by yourself, unbearable to wake up
to another lonely morning.
There are so many things you want to say, conversations
you planned with the one who left you behind,
but you keep the words to yourself, the words so painful
they'll cut your tongue bloody if you speak them.
Even now, it hurts.

Grief isn't a neat and simple thing.
There are no flowers that could lighten your heart,
not enough wine to fill the hole in your ribcage.
You'll have to amputate a part of yourself just to survive,
a private offering to the grief, a sacrifice heavily paid.

You don't think you can go on, but you do.
You survive, even when you think you can't,
you do.

OCEAN OF SALT

Restless legs and anxious fingers
twist and shift,
trying to be comfortable
in your own skin.

The yawning chasm
between giving up, or giving in,
grows in your chest,
threatening to swallow you whole.

THE INSOMNIACS CLUB

Insomnia is a bug crawling on your skin,
biting and gnawing at your flesh,
an itch you can never scratch.

So you sit on your bed,
sheets tangled around you,
a grand display
of the mess you've become.
Hair wet with sweat, you cry,
wishing you could close your eyes
and dream of fireworks.

But even this peace evades you,
out of your reach.
Sleep won't come, not to you,
and you wonder,
is there a club of insomniacs
who sit on their bed and cry,
who can share in your loneliness
and eat wormwood for breakfast?

DESTROY YOURSELF

We hate ourselves
because it is easier than love.

We pick apart our flaws
because it is easier than acceptance.

We destroy ourselves
because it is easier than living.

We hide away
because it is safer than taking risks.

We give up our dreams
because it is easier than reaching for them.

We use excuses
because it is easier to hide behind them.

We turn away from ourselves
because it is easier than facing
what we've become.

THE DICHOTOMY OF BEING HERE AND BEING GONE

There are days when you wonder
how much longer must you go on
before giving up.

There are days spent sleeping
in the arms of madness,
hours walking around your bedroom
and talking to the walls.

With the clock ticking away,
a reminder of lost time
and a muted television
keeping you from being alone,
you try to make it through another day
of this bitter war against your brain.

Do you go on, only to make it through
another day of being ill?

Or do you give in, admit defeat
and close your eyes,
pretending you aren't here?

SHRINE

How do you honour the grief
of losing the ones you love
when you've spent lifetimes
digging them up,
only to bury them
again
and
again
and
again?

ONE DAY AT A TIME

Relapsing is expected.
We never fully let go of our old selves,
folding them into pebbles
and placing them in our pockets,
carrying their weight with us
wherever we go.
Even if we let go, they never let go of us.
We can never fully get over our addictions,
we just learn to live with them.

FAITHFUL DISCONSOLATION

Quagmire shoes and unsteady knees,
shaking hands and sweaty palms,
words stuck on a dry tongue.
Pointless beginnings and unravelling goodbyes,
friends turned strangers,
shadows left behind from turned backs.
Ghosts echo against the walls,
voices of imaginary friends become a comfort,
and aloneness is no longer.

ALONE

You are missing from your own life.
The thought cuts into you,
but you are so far gone and overwhelmed,
you don't know how to change.

There used to be invitations,
others wanting to be around you,
fighting for your attention.

Then you disappeared,
and the invitations dried up,
the people around you no longer smiled
or looked pleased to see you.

You are a burden, a vampire
sucking the joy and life from them.

They are done with you,
and you realize,
you are done with yourself.

DOUBTFUL

You live in your room,
in your bed,
in your mind,
the world leaving you behind.

You've written your story,
erased yourself from it,
unsure where you belong.

The loneliness called to you
and despite yourself,
you went to it,

wrapping your arms
around its jagged edges.
And you try to hold onto hope,

but you are riddled with doubts.
Will there ever be a day
when you are better?

YOUNGBLOOD

Young and lonely, desperate to be seen,
to leave this nowhere town
with dreams too big for your body
and endless possibilities that steal your breath.

Every second is a second too late,
and the longer you linger here, the further you are
from who you want to be and where you want to go.

The fear of failure whispers in your ear,
an itch you can't reach, filling you with dread,
and you worry, maybe, just maybe,
you'll become everything you're scared of.

Giving up in defeat,
never saying what you really feel,
settling for mediocrity, settling for nothing,
losing purpose and floating by.

You're scared of growing old, stuck here
in this nowhere town,
afraid of being content to make a home
at the bottom of the pit.

PILLOW THOUGHTS II

orphaned memories
laugh
in the quietest
of silences

DEPRESSION

Depression is
greasy hair and stained pyjamas,
hiding in solitude
and wondering why it tastes so good.

Depression is
easy smiles and flat eyes
then crawling back home
and making a fort in exhaustion.

Depression is
comfortable and uncomfortable,
a home and a cage.

Depression is
sleeping too much, or not at all,
eating until round, or a skeletal frame.

Depression is
wondering if your cinderblock feet
will carry your weight
or pull you down into an ocean of shame.

WINTER

We live on the edge
of madness and sanity,
on the precipice
of yet another breakdown.

Vigilant,
so vigilant,
always waiting and waiting
for the vines to slip
around our ankles
and pull us down.

Do we bloom
with the seasons
or wither
in our winter's sadness?

LOST IN HEALING

When you are ill, you wonder
what it means to be whole.
What will that look like,
to wake up with the sun
instead of greasy, knotted hair
and bloodshot eyes?

When you are in recovery, you wonder
when you will be sick again,
missing your broken heart
and a head of madness.

In your illness, you found an identity,
but in your healing, you lost yourself.

CLAUSTROPHOBIC LOVE

They place their expectations on you,
that you're getting better
and are back to normal,
whatever your normal was.

You're a ticking time bomb,
knowing it's just a matter of time
before you'll implode again.

You're isolated in your illness,
missing from your life,
reduced to an echo of yourself.

But you're showing up
and that's all they see,
thinking you've recovered,
your illness miraculously cured.

They mean well,
their intentions based on love,
but it's claustrophobic,
their expectations are a straitjacket
holding you hostage, a shadow

following you around.

If only they'd understand
that you need them to see you
for all that you are—
dishevelled and ill,
or recovered and in bloom.

But you keep this struggle to yourself,
not wanting to disappoint them,
and you drown in the pressure
of the love they give you.

EQUATION

There
is
no
truth
here.

Unless
sadness
is
the
truth.

HERE IS THE CATCH-22

You want to disappear
from the world, from your life,
but you don't want to let go
just yet.

You want the hurt to go away,
to make it all stop,
but you don't want
the ones who love you
to hurt.

So you exist
in the grey in-between
of leaving or staying,

and it's like this,
you settle on just getting by,
day by day,

and when the season changes,
you wonder,
why haven't you?

MONSTROUS

There is solitude
in your illness
and the people you love
may not understand,
wondering
why you've become
this twisted little thing.

DREAMING AWAY

We dream

because it is easier

than living.

ROSE-TINTED GLASSES

Your illness
took so much from you
and you grieve
for everything you lost.
The grief scrapes
away your guts,
and this false nostalgia
for a life dreamt
is just another way
to make yourself hurt.

EVEN TOGETHER, WE'RE FAR APART

Straining tree branch fingertips,
grasping,
but we're still alone.

FRIENDS TURNED STRANGERS

You oscillate between
synthetic aloneness and crowded loneliness,
and soon the invitations wither away
as the seasons change,
summer leaves mottled and rotten
from the winter of your sadness.

Now when you're together,
it's a simple transaction
of their cherry-kissed smiles and words
plucked from your grim mouth,
and you try to hide the knotted skin
between your brows
and the mantle of sadness
on your sloping shoulders.

You speak in monosyllables,
but their ears hear an opera
of counterfeited happiness
you've spent years perfecting,
the air witnessing a slaughter of friendship
turned acquaintances.

Inevitably,
their outstretched hands
turn into disappointed fists,
and they pull back from you,
once together, now apart.
Your friends stop coming around
and you crawl back home, beneath your blanket
of aloneness, seeking the hot spring of sleep.

There is no consolation,
losing your friends to your illness.
And despite yourself,
you've become disconnected,
choosing imaginary friends over them.

GLASSINE WORDS

The weight of their words sticks to you,
fingerprints on your bones,
wash, scrub, soak,
but the letters strung together in love
are tattooed in the folds of your brain.
And the sharp edges cut
into your palms as you grasp them,
holding on
when you should've let go.

THE GRACE IN BEING SAD

It's okay to not be okay,
to take a step back,
throw up your arms and say,
No, I give up.
I don't want to go on,
I try and try,
but what's the point?

Be damaged and defeated and be okay with that.
Rest in your sadness, just for a little while,
telling yourself,
I'll rest only until I have the energy
to pull myself back together again.

There is nothing wrong with falling apart
and shattering into tiny little pieces.
Take ownership in falling down,
find grace in not knowing what you want
or who you are.

There is peace in your brokenness,
a chance to find your footing,
a place where you can speak without shame.

Be open with yourself and with others
about your mental illness,
that you're not doing okay,
and that's okay.

Who cares if they don't understand you?
You don't need their understanding
because you accept your broken self.

You accept that you're down,
accept it'll take a while
to pull yourself together again,
and you accept the uncertainty of it all.
There is freedom here.

CADMEAN VICTORY

There are misunderstandings that end in tears,
quilled words and barbed tongues,
tornado arguments and lashing words.

We try and try, but still,
we speak different languages,
finding faults in the silence,
hurt embedded in our mistranslations.

We only hear antonyms
to every spoken word,
emphasized in the growing arena
between our mouths.

UNWELL

You tell them you are not well, depressed and mad.
They blame you for your illness,
saying you choose to live like this.

You tell them you are ill, insomniac and manic.
They sing songs of worry,
but their melody is flat and hollow.

You tell them you will always be stuck
in the quicksand of your mind.
They say it is your fault for being depressed.

But do they know what it means
when your guts are unwell
but your face is clean and pristine?

SLEEPING AWAY

There are days
when you force yourself
to go back to sleep,
pretending the world
doesn't spin without you,
and you can get lost
in the dreams
of true love, and self-love,
and not wake up to this.

THE MOURNING

You were too busy writing loneliness in the sky
and kicking sandcastles into crashing waves
to look around at the emptiness of your life
and realize how much you've missed.

BLUE

If you aren't your sadness
then who are you?

There will come a day
when being blue
is not enough,

and you'll try
to let go of the sadness,
but it won't let go of you.

IMPOSTOR

You sewed yourself together
with threads of madness,
spent so long being ill
that people think
this is your new normal.
And when you try to heal and recover,
painfully picking apart the threads,
they hold you back
wondering who the hell you've become,
so used to you being gone.

PINK ELEPHANT

They tiptoe around you, not wanting to upset
your balance of walking across a tightrope.
They wrangle back words of concern and annoyance,
wanting you to abandon your pity party of one.

But they don't want to be the reason
that you fall from the edge. It is this carefulness,
and keen eyes that look away,
sullen silence and barbed frowns,
that eats and eats at you.

The pink elephant in the room
becomes blinding and large, and not even you
can ignore it any longer. With a snap
of your fingers, you wish everyone would act
as they did before your fall, and no one
would tap dance around you anymore.

You would rather they speak
instead of biting the tips of their tongues,
holding back their hurricane words.
If only they would trust your strength
not to fall apart again.

TEETH

You try to cut yourself apart
and excavate your skin.
Will there be answers in your bones,
reasons to live in your veins?
This becomes an addiction, the screaming
red lines on the plains of your skin,
a biting sting, a sudden reprieve.

And when you try to stop, you miss
the ritual of release, but you know
you can't go back to the butcher's block.
You're missing too many limbs,
you're no longer whole.

So you put away the metal teeth
in a makeshift coffin, burying them your closet.
You can't bear to throw away this lifeline
that has carried you this far, a friend, a saviour,
helping you get through another day.

You carry this shameful secret in your pocket
and it becomes yet another addiction,
though you don't reach for the teeth.

There is peace in knowing it's waiting for you,
an old friend, this foe of yours.

In the early days of giving up this habit,
you count the hours, unwilling to give in.
The hours turn into days,
and the days bleed into months. Soon,
you are counting in victory,
finding pride in being clean,

and you realize, you don't need a crutch
to get through the days.
You have found strength within you,
away from the metal teeth,
you will make it through the days
in defiance and courage.

STARSTRUCK

In the lull of night,
under the blanket of the moon,
you lie awake,
staring at the sky,
wondering if there will come a day
when you will shine brighter
than the stars.

HOPE FOR THE HOPELESS

You're afraid to let go
of the melancholic darkness
you've held onto for so long,
making it into who you are.

You held on
when you should've let go,
fearful of the light, terrified of hope.
You've spent years building a castle
atop your gloom. It's all you've ever known,
a habit and an addiction, a crutch and a comfort.

You wonder,
if you let go of the darkness, will you become
blinded by the light, losing your experience
forged from walking through hurricanes?
You don't want to become
an advertisement for a Stepford life,
a generic uplifting poster, mass produced.

Slowly,
one step at a time,

you let go of the darkness,
and in the absence of darkness,

you remain,
not blinded by the sunshine
but not lost in the hurricane.

YOU ARE NOT WEAK FOR NEEDING HELP

You thought you could do this on your own,
but there comes a day when you falter
and you seek help, needing a lifejacket,
a buoy to keep you afloat.

You grapple with the quiet shame
of needing help just to get by,
but you sought help,
and you slowly get better,
the sea of shame in which you swim,
easing into a river of gratefulness.

There are no miracles tumbling from the sky.
You won't suddenly wake up
to find yourself different from the night before.
It's slow and painful, a study in patience,
but you'll get there, one day at a time.

THE FINERY OF HOPE

You made a home in your loneliness and gloom,
wearing melancholic pearls and teardrop earrings,
a fur coat skinned from your illness,
and you wore it with pride,
showcasing your finery for all to see.

But you're tired of being the Queen of Sadness,
so you let go of the trinkets of brokenness,
tearing the sadness from your skin,
leaving gaps in your body,
and you wonder,
how can you ever fill the absences in you?

But you are determined to build yourself a home
not built from sadness and weeping wounds,
but carved from strength and unwavering courage.
Now you want to make a home
in sunny times and cautious hope.

COMING ALIVE

A trench exists between you and life,
filled with paths not taken and paths overlooked,
your life, a battlefield
of times lost and times long gone.
Who you were before the war
is not who you are now.

There are those who stayed,
scarred but still with you,
and there are those who left,
unable to understand the warring in your head.

You blamed yourself
for not being good enough,
ashamed that your illness
turned you into this.

You flicker back and forth
between self-loathing and desperation,
waiting for a day when you'll get better.

It's just you now,
stuck in your quicksand mind,

and as you stare at the ceiling above you,
you hold hope in the palm of your hands,
telling yourself, *I will make it out of this alive.*

Hurt and damaged,
but alive.

CORPOREAL

All you want is for someone to see
the grotesque shadow of sadness
strung on a leash behind you.

But the ones who love you,
fear you getting lost in the melee
of melancholy.

They don't share in your madness
or understand what it means
to be damaged and weathered,
a messy tornado of a life falling apart,
a hurricane brewing under your skin.

You are beyond the reach
of their fingertips, and in your otherness,
there will be those who see you.

You belong, here and now,
you are heard, you are understood,
you are seen.

REPRIEVE

You are depressed,
not fragile
or broken.
You are resting
for a day
when you will climb
out of this hole.

ACKNOWLEDGMENTS

Thank you to my editors, Anna McDonnell Dowling and Misti Wolanski. You both worked so hard and dedicated yourselves to helping me polish off this collection of poems. I couldn't have done it without you both. Thank you.

Bố, thank you for being my lighthouse; I love you more than you'll ever know.

Thank you to my friends for not giving up on me and being present when even I wasn't there. I love you.

Thank you, dear reader, for holding this collection in your hands. I hope it helps you, I hope you know you are not alone in this struggle, and I hope you are practicing self-care. Take care of yourself.

Survive and endure,

Annie Sophie Le

www.anniesophiele.com
Instagram: @anniesophiele

www.ingramcontent.com/pod-product-compliance
Lightning Source LLC
Chambersburg PA
CBHW020913080526
44589CB00011B/571